MW01281798

CRANE

Crane

Tessa Bolsover

Black Ocean
Boston · Chicago

Black Ocean
P.O. Box 52030
Boston, MA 02205
blackocean.org

Cover design by Janaka Stucky | janakastucky.com
Cover photograph by Tessa Bolsover

ISBN: 978-1-965154-03-8

Library of Congress Control Number: 2025931119

Printed in Canada

FIRST EDITION

Contents

CRANE

Tear pages from a calendar
scatter them into sunshine and snow

—Susan Howe

The moths that clung to the door were translucent enough to let through a dust of light when the dawn sun crested in across the ceiling (stained) to carve an arc over the books, my bed. All moths die of hunger, you told me once; I didn't know then where you'd read this. You said the larvae eat ravenously before closing themselves in chrysalis, after which they never eat again. Do they drink? I asked. You did not know.

"Life is death we're lengthy at, death the hinge to life," wrote Emily Dickinson in a letter to her cousins Fanny and Louisa in 1863. This chiasmic image of a life/death axis is reminiscent of the Roman deity Janus, who, gate-like, sees both forward and backward at once. In Ovid's *Fasti*, Janus comes across a huntress nymph—variously called Crane, Cardea, or Carna—in a forest grove. Evading his attempt to seduce her, she pretends to follow him into a cave before darting away to hide in the woods. Janus, able to see behind his back, catches and rapes her. He then places a whitethorn twig into her hand, giving her power over hinges. She lives on as the little-known goddess of hinges and protector of children and houses.

Hinges connect and hold apart. They set a frame in which separate components open and close while remaining a single object. Hinges are the points at which a structure undoes itself; they allow a plane to fold, collapse, and open into space while maintaining the possibility for multiplicity and mutability. Language behaves similarly: the unsaid within the said lends a word both its particularity and its instability. There are voids in the architecture of writing—moth bites in the weave of language. The unsaid pushes up against the curves and notches of lettering.

Cardea, from **Cardo**, ĭnis, m. cf. **κράδη**, to swing; Sanscr. kurd, a spring, a leap . . . *the hinge of a door* or *gate . . . mechanical beams that fit together; a mortise, axe-shaped tenon, dovetail . . .* In garlands, *the place where two ends interfold . . .* In astronomy, *the point about which something turns, a pole . . . A line limiting the field, drawn through from north to south . . .* the mountain Taurus, *line or limit . . . Of the four cardinal points . . . Of the earth as the centre of the universe,* acc. to the belief of the ancients . . . *Of the intersection of inclined surfaces . . . Of winter solstice . . . Of the pivotal point* or *circumstance . . . in so critical a moment*

κράδη
quivering spray at the end of a branch

to suffer from blight

In Ovid's *Fasti*, Cardea's story is fused with that of Carna, a protective deity of vital organs. A scene is recounted in which Cardea or Carna—collapsed into one—protects a young child who'd been attacked by vampiric screech owls, called *strix*. She enters the room of the dying infant, marks the doorposts with sprigs of whitethorn, and pours a tincture across the threshold. Then, holding the intestines of a piglet, she offers its life as a sacrifice for the child's. The boy grows up to be Procas, king of Alba Longa and great-grandfather to Romulus and Remus, the twin founders of Rome.

The conflation of Cardea and Carna (derived from *caro*, meaning "flesh" or "meat") was likely intentional. Ovid was a trickster; he caught sight of a link in the two women's stories and polluted the boundaries between them, entangling their contours to enfold new layers of meaning. Transitions between myths and figures are frequently blurred in the *Fasti*, echoing the poet's wider engagement with the theme of mutability. "Bodies . . . are always, restlessly, changing," a counterfeit Pythagoras reflects in book XV of the *Metamorphoses*. "Nothing keeps its own form, and Nature, the renewer of things, refreshes one shape from another. Believe me, nothing dies in the universe as a whole, but it varies and changes its aspect . . . the total sum is constant."

Ovid's writing, though widely popular during his life, was judged by Augustus to be subversive and immoral, and in 8 CE the poet was exiled from Rome. He gave only a brief explanation of the reason for his expulsion: "carmen et error," a poem and an error. The poem likely refers to his controversial *Ars Amatoria* (*The Art of Love*); what the error was we do not know. He was sent to a settlement at the furthest margin of the empire, in modern-day Romania, where he spent the rest of his life.

Anne Carson calls poetry "the willful creation of error." Errors unravel the edges of things held separate. The lines upholding the parameters of individual entities are disrupted, run awry. To err is to wander astray into the heresy of uncertainty. There are no further mentions of Crane's skill for hunting or of the grove where she slept beneath a latticework of leaves.

I want to say that Crane, too, is double-sided, Gemini. In Ovid's violent telling, it is as though she slips out of her own story just after the moment of her capture—there is a sudden pivot and we find ourselves abruptly in another myth, in another setting, with another Crane. There are violences we learn to wear like eyes on the backs of our heads

κράδη
theatric device for suspending actors in midair

a type of crane

Every morning on my way to work I watch the dawn stream past the bus windows and feel a thin wire of sensation passing through my body, connecting me to the sparse scattering of passengers, asleep or reading, as we race through a long blue throb of snow. Encapsulated in metal, on our separate routes, in the momentary stasis between night and day, public and private, life and work. Our breath clinging to the windows in frosty pools.

I do not want to draw equivalencies, but to place objects beside one another and witness how a surface shimmers in and out of form and loss itself. Before work some days I walk to the canal to watch the rungs of rust striating its edges phase into vibrant color. I imagine Crane down below, pushing through the reeds in too-big boots, the pigment-silt beneath the shallows billowing around her feet in copper clouds.

her vision the
        Grass

                             (a place to be concrete)

; *line limiting the field, drawn*
from north to south

        (vocative)   dips its pendulum—

Thresholds are a space of complication between crossings—the sill between life and death, night and day, sleep and waking. Desiring bodies, reading bodies, bodies of text—each crosses the boundaries of the self to reach another. Like doors we thrum, latch, fold, are thrown open into light.

Three other writers mention Cardea in ancient texts. In the fifth century, Macrobius wrote that a temple was dedicated to her by Brutus, who credited the goddess for his successful deception of the Tarquins. During the Roman Empire's shift to Christianity, Augustine wrote numerous attacks on polytheism, and in one of them passingly cites Cardea alongside two other minor deities—Forculus (from *fores*, "door") and Limentinus (from *limen*, "threshold")—chiding the polytheists for needing three gods to guard a single doorway. Tertullian, another forefather of Christian theology, references the trio of threshold gods in his treatises *Of the Soldier's Crown* and *Of Idolatry*. The latter begins similarly to Augustine's before veering into a philosophical statement on the dangerous emptiness of names:

> "There are among the Romans even gods of entrances; Cardea (Hinge-goddess), called after hinges, and Forculus (Door-god) after doors, and Limentinus (Threshold-god) after the threshold, and Janus himself (Gate-god) after the gate: and of course we know that, though names be empty and feigned, when they are drawn down into superstition, demons and every unclean spirit seize them for themselves, through the bond of consecration."

There is an affinity between names and thresholds, both of which enact the dangers of nonfixity. Doors delineate the porous boundaries between one space and another, sustaining both an architecture and its holes. As symbols of flux, they are riddled with idols. Both "empty" and "unclean," their multidirectionality may be threatening to the linearity of imperialist thought. Unguarded, thresholds permit a flow of exit and entry, and create a space for dwelling in between. Names, too, exist in a between-space, in two rooms at once, subject to multiple meanings and unconsecrated creakings. Often they let in more than their user intends.

Noon, between shifts. The buildings are alert with angles.
Nouns loosen their attachment to a referent. Loose sheets of
photo paper leaked to sun

In *The Neutral*, Roland Barthes claims that to describe is to unthread a word. He quotes Voltaire: "Newton *a parfile* {unthreaded} the sun's light, as our ladies *parfilent* {unthread} a cloth of gold . . . to unweave it thread by thread to separate out the gold." A decade earlier, Barthes asserted that we should not attempt to decipher texts but disentangle them. "The structure can be followed, 'run' (like the thread of a stocking) at every point and at every level, but there is nothing beneath." A textile is an intricate web of material relations. The same is true of texts. To unthread a cloth you must follow the individual fibers, the branching dendrons of nuance. There is no essence of a word hidden beneath its infinite readings, though we simplify. The dye remains locked in the thread.

I awake and the boughs, battered and paddling against the window, bruise shadows in the hardwood. Amplified by rain, the sounds inside resonate like pieces of a disassembled object. Slowly, words begin to spread with a viscous clarity over everything. Words unstruck, simple as honey, invoking all that is secret and unprivatized. In the predawn haze I wash my face, still printed with the fresh tracks of a dream in which I'm standing on the side of a mountain, the bare slopes covered with small white rocks that rearrange their matter slowly beneath my feet.

Elsewhere in *The Neutral*, Barthes describes three stages of suspension. The first is the nonreply. The second, stammering: "to evade not the reply but the nonreply." The third he calls the dilatory—a method rooted in the hope that the question will be forgotten, that the demand will shift. "The essence of the dilatory is its desire to be infinite."

Sleep threads its way deeper into my days, carving tributaries through waking life like runs in nylon, only visible from certain angles. Dreams pass between the nodding heads of the women on the dawn bus, which loll like heavy flowers caught in wind. I watch the slowly shifting patterns of condensation on the windows, fingers lightly grazing the metal seat, the tight loops of thread along the borders of my sleeves.

Early spring. At the transfer station, I step onto a subway car and find the ads have been spray-painted blue. Focusing my eyes, I can trace faint outlines of obscured images beneath: the curve of a shoulder, the sharp edges of illegible block lettering. I am held, momentarily, in a rickety suspension between stops, a moving room of false windows. Mimetic distance wavering blue like plastic bags, like the base of a flame

Calendar pages soaked and used as bean sieve

I awake each day knowing little

Hold the pieces careful
ly Crane said (in dream)   the glimmer nouns   All

light escaped from other empires

That language slips through its own gaps does not diminish its material impact. Language (creaking) overflows itself and yet it's used to control, cordon, and capture. Words fold out and back and forward into history. How crystals formed in caves enclose infinitudes of edges, expanding in the same breath that they condense. "Words do not hang on the façade of the present, advertising their availability. They are embedded in history, which forms no continuous tradition" (Susan Buck-Morss).

Reeds bent to wind flicker past the train windows in a patch-worked flame of motion. Refracted light appears brighter when broken up into a shimmer. Touch it with a name and step back quickly. As a painter I was taught to squint my eyes to isolate the composition. To blur the details. Some say reading requires a similar technique: one must strip away the words to sense what's underneath. Invariably we find we're latched to words, held in and by their weave. Each vocable wreathed in "a halo of possible meanings" (Barthes); clanging with significations, power relations, histories.

In *Discrepant Engagement*, Nathaniel Mackey invokes the "creaking of the word"—the Dogon name for weaving blocks, the bases upon which their looms rest—as a way of considering the elusive, shifting foundations of language. Just as the negative space between fibers is intrinsic to weaving, a creak is the byproduct of a vacancy within or between shifting materials. "That language creaks," Mackey writes, "testifies to the rickety, telltale base on which its word-weave, its 'fabrication,' rests." It is "the noise upon which the word is based, the discrepant foundation of all coherence and articulation, of the purchase upon the world fabrication affords."

in legible silk

freckled lens   folds open moment

ary
          vertigo of stasis

          count the breath's

       incisions into stone

Early on in Ovid's description of Crane, he describes her method for circumventing the unwanted attention of men: feigning interest, she instructs them to lead her to a secluded cave and, while their backs are turned, slips away to hide among the plants and boulders. As a form of self-protection, she disappears by camouflaging into her environment. Many moths and other insects evade predators by visually merging with their habitat, blurring the boundaries between themselves and their surroundings. There's the *Griposia aprilina* moth, whose wing patterns blend seamlessly into lichen-flecked bark, and the *Oxydia*, whose variegated brown wings, when paused amid plants, create the illusion of a dead leaf. Mantises become nearly invisible among leaves and branches; some even hide as budding twigs in early bloom. There are butterfly species that disguise themselves as predators: the *Trochilium* has evolved to look and sound like a wasp, while the lower wings of the *Caligo*, or "owl butterfly," bare large, yellow-rimmed eyespots set within feather-like ripples of ivory and brown. With its wings outstretched, the *Caligo*'s curved abdomen is reminiscent of a beak.

"Morphological mimicry," writes Roger Caillois, "could be, after the fashion of chromatic mimicry, an actual photography . . . a reproduction in three-dimensional space with solids and voids." The mimic melds with its surroundings, undermining the distinction between self and non, original and duplicate.

"It is with represented space that the drama becomes specific, since the living creature, the organism, is no longer the origin of the coordinates, but one point among others." The mimetic being parts the boundaries of the self to slip into the wider web of place.

In the body there are doorways. Standing on the M train platform, a rush of wind flickers my clothes and I feel a sudden longing for something I cannot name but which adheres itself to the sea of silvery roofs, soft with age and rain, the green shatter of a Heineken bottle. Light settles on the coat of the woman beside me as her palms slowly curve to face the air like secret flowers turning to an unmarked sun.

Seeking departure. Seeking weaker points of crossing. Seeking radio, hyacinth. The minerality of green, delay expanse. Seeking variations in marigold, in flight pattern. A broken turnstile, silt dawning over concrete, you know an edge is only tilted field

Half-asleep on an empty train, I see Crane again in dream, her face blurred as though photographed in motion. What is vivid: a single glitter lodged between the moving eyes, the determined comma-crease at the edge of her mouth. The sky slides along the window in striations of blue and green. The sound of blood aligns with the sound of the train, the ear, the air. All minerals alight with magnetism double-imaged

coin (creaking
comb tooth broken

                        Loup cipher

                        grove of exit
                        sun Bodiless
                        when sang

Each morning at dawn I pass the metal crane outside the bank, suspended midair, the total stillness of a stage set. The dimensionality of morning light gives sight itself a kind of depth, like softened metal.

Early spring. I dip my hand into the canal, sifting water; green bubbles just below the surface crest and cling like beetles to the rocks. Error weaves into the frame, softening that which had been calcified. Error like the roots that dislodge fences, error like grass.

Do I lay it down among the shallows. The silver floral switchblade my mother gave me. The jointed clip you slipped into my pocket. Lay it softly in the silt and watch the surface shimmer

DELAY FIGURE

In Ovid's *Metamorphoses*, the story of Echo and Narcissus begins with a premonition from the blind sage Tiresias. When asked if the then-infant Narcissus would live a long life, he replies: "If he knows himself—not." Sixteen years later, while hunting deer, Narcissus is spotted by Echo, a nymph cursed to speak only by repeating the ends of others' phrases. Watching Narcissus move through the woods, she is overtaken by longing. Unable to speak to him, she follows him in secret, sounding out the edges of his words. When she finally emerges from the foliage to embrace him, he winces away angrily. Ashamed, Echo retreats into the darkness of a cave where, sleepless and hungry, her body slowly dissolves until only her voice remains.

Other rejected lovers of Narcissus shared similar fates. One day, a broken-hearted boy prays that Narcissus "may himself love as I have loved him . . . without obtaining his beloved." Out hunting, Narcissus stops to drink from a pool of clear water and becomes riveted to his reflection. Hypnotized, his desperation grows in the feedback loop of his unsubstantiated desire; he is unable to touch his reflection, nor to look away. Suspended there in love and grief, exhausted and malnourished, he and his reflection pale and weaken. "Alas, dear boy, whom I have vainly cherished," he laments. Echo—bodiless, listening—returns his words. "Farewell," he says; "*Farewell*," rings Echo back.

His head droops heavy into grasses before resurfacing as flowers. This is how Ovid's story goes. But I'm not as concerned with Narcissus, or the fulfilling of his prophesy, as I am with Echo's slow decentering, her voice's deep collusion with the woods. How, in longing she. A voice or current pulled in all directions. Begins to voice nonhuman things..

*

"Relation contaminates, sweetens, as a principle, or as flower dust," writes Édouard Glissant. Tides, hauling and shifting on cords. The moon resounds in partial tones.

Re-sound. To pull apart and echo back. Synthesize the space between. In dissonant relation, un-strung voice unfinished figure of delay.

*

Alone, in caves, Echo takes apart her body and readheres to soundwaves. Unfolds every angle of a touch. Transgressing the finite limits of the individual body, she disperses into her environment, recast as a figural *sound body*—defined by Deborah Kapchan as "a resonant body that is porous, that transforms according to the vibrations of its environment and correspondingly transforms that environment . . . unloosening thereby the knotted dualisms of nature/culture, human/nonhuman, body/mind." Scattered selves dismantle centers. When the sovereignty of the closed-off individual is disturbed so too is the scaffold of dualisms erected by Western thought to uphold it. Echo passes from a sequestered self into an ecology of relations, from one voice into choral rounds.

*

Reflections do not sleep. Echo and Narcissus' separate changes double back in looped insomnia. Worrying the seams. What food is it that holds us to our prior forms?

*

Though she's primarily known for her unrequited love of Narcissus, Echo appears in an array of classical texts, most of which situate her in relation to Pan, the satyr god of shepherds, wilderness, and improvisational music. These references, usually brief, recount Pan's unreciprocated love for her—or, arguably, for her ability to imitate the sound of his own music, reflected through her "secret voice."

In the second century, Echo appears in Longus' *Daphnis and Chloe* as an Orpheus-like figure—a talented musician whose body is torn into pieces. In the poem, Longus describes a scene in which the young protagonist Chloe hears an echo for the first time: the sound of rowing fishermen refracted in a crescent bay. To explain the phenomenon, Daphnis tells her the story of Echo, a nymph with extraordinary musical talents who became the object of Pan's desire. When she rejected his advances, Pan—jealous of her singing voice and enraged by her refusal—drove a group of shepherds into hysteria and incited them to tear Echo apart, scattering the remnants of her body. Gaia, watching, hid the pieces carefully, preserving their ability to sing.

*

In Ovid's version, Echo dissolves the boundaries of her self in longing. In Longus', she is torn apart for her lack of it. The double standard glints a ready trap. "Relation comprehends violence, marks its distance," writes Glissant. To map an echo. is to map a field of impacts, the haptic refractions of unequally distributed touch.

*

"The Western metaphysical and linguistic traditions have bequeathed us two powerful ideas about voice," Amanda Weidman states. "One is the idea of voice as guarantor of truth and self-presence, from which springs the familiar idea that the voice expresses self and identity, and that agency consists in having a voice. This is coupled with the idea that the sonic and material aspects of the voice are separable from and subordinate to its referential content or message . . . such a model treats the sonic, material aspects of voice as secondary and as potentially disruptive to the sovereignty of the subject." As Weidman goes on to emphasize, the imagined split between "signifying voice" and non-referential "vocality" is embedded in many of the West's longstanding binaries:

"human versus animal; language versus music; male versus female. The female voice has played a particularly important role in Western cultural production as a vehicle for presenting inarticulate vocality."

By integrating into and voicing the non-human environment, Echo disrupts the standard limits of the individual body as a "guarantor of self-presence," as well as the concept of purely significatory language. Through her indiscriminate mediation of both human and non-human sounds, referential and non-referential alike, she simultaneously gives voice to that which is generally considered incapable of having one (falling stones, rushing water, machine noise, animal sounds), while in the same gesture distorting the sovereignty of the "signifying"— distinctly human, predominately white and masculine—voice.

*

The voice gathers wood. Quarter moon wavers on a rockface, hues deleted by the dark. In the excess curve of falling things, a sound takes shape. Simulated hush of air's displacement. What is it that gets carried in the space between two soundings? Sonar image, object mirror ringing holes in darkness. A longing framed as self then repossessed.

*

In bat and sea mammal communities, echolocation is used to navigate in low light. Short, high-frequency ultrasonic tones are projected into space; upon contact with a body or object the waves reflect back, allowing the echolocating creature to create an aural map of its immediate environment.

Shapes in dimness curve in audible hold. During the First and Second World Wars, sonar technologies were developed to aid in underwater navigation and naval warfare. Emulating the biological transmission and reception of sound waves by bats and toothed whales, sonar transducers emit a series of beam-shaped sound waves underwater and measure the time it takes for the sound to reflect from the surface of objects and return to the receiver.

Ship and submarine sonar has damaging impacts on marine ecology—particularly on sea mammals who rely on echolocation to survive. The military cooptation of echolocation led to increased levels of stranding and disorientation among the sea creatures from which the hydroacoustic technology was appropriated.

*

In *A Thousand Plateaus*, Deleuze and Guattari describe the sonorous refrain as having territorial origins: "The bird sings to mark its territory," they write. "Forces of chaos, terrestrial forces, cosmic forces: all of these confront each other and converge in the territorial refrain." The refrain's claim on property, however, is undermined by its own articulation. "There is a margin of deterritorialization affecting the territory itself. There is a series of unclaspings." An echo simultaneously marks and transgresses borders. A sound emitted from a source collides with the physical boundaries of a terrestrial place—cliff face, hallway, nave—sonorizing all that it can touch. But really it's the space between that's sonorized; a sonority that leaks, spills over. The sound is taken up by something other than what voiced it, jeopardizing the authority of the "original" and the imagined centrality of its position in space and time. Sound overflows its utterance, emphasizing its material relationality. The emitted sound refracts an image of its environment and in the same instant is unclasped, distorted, estranged from itself.

*

The western scrub jay is one of few birds known to enact rituals following the death of its kind. When one finds another dead it begins to sing—a strange wailing sound that beckons other jays to form a ring of noise around the dead. After they disperse, none will be found feeding or collecting nest materials in the area for two to three days.

Within sound there is voice. Within voice, speech. Voice forms a membrane around a word, a ring of noise. Its tonal nuances bind sound with meaning; signification and sonic materiality are revealed as both indebted to and in excess of one another.

*

Music has long troubled the edge between the linguistic and nonlinguistic significations of sound. In the essay "Cante Moro," Nathaniel Mackey describes the blues musician Mississippi Fred McDowell's use of voice and slide guitar as blurring the line between speech and nonspeech. For Mackey, this dialogical yet not necessarily lexical quality, common in Black music, is inlaid with "some kind of dissatisfaction with—if not critique of—the limits of conventionally articulate, verbal speech. One of the reasons the music so often goes over into nonspeech—moaning, humming, shouts, nonsense lyrics, scat—is to say, among other things, that the realm of conventionally articulate speech is not sufficient for saying what needs to be said . . . What you can say, what can be stated within the limits of conventionally articulate speech, is not enough. What you need is this *sound*."

*

When Orpheus was torn apart by frenzied Bacchae on the banks of the Hebrus River, his lyre and severed head floated for days downstream and was received as an oracle. As Gaia collected Echo's scattered limbs, the pieces were still "quivering with song." It's unlikely that the connection between music and dismemberment in these two stories is coincidental. Elsewhere in "Cante Moro," Mackey describes a saxophone solo played by Sonny Rollins by blowing only into the detached mouthpiece, "sans horn." Mackey notes,

44

"again, we have separation, severance, amputation . . . the idea of music as a phantom limb, a phantom reach with/ after something you have but do not have. It is a kind of re-membering, a mended dismemberment."

*

The experience of time, some say, is not an objective facet of the world but our species' mechanism for reconciling with entropy. What changes between repetitions is not time so much as one's own dissolution. An echo is refrain marked by decay.

Sound takes the shape of an event at the same moment it transforms, echoes back a field of losses. "To varying degrees," writes Mark M. Smith, an echo is "a faded facsimile of an original sound, a reflection of time passed." On the radio I heard someone say that memories degrade a little more each time they're recalled, that each act of remembrance mediates and loosens the memory's attachment to a source. "A work of mourning is an exercise in forgetting," said David Wills. "Which is the memory, and which is the forgetting?"

Feel your way along the sandstone strata hearing distance. Place your ear against the water's surface. "There. Messages flow through clear lake water and yes, gravity pulls matter together to form a cosmic web" (Susan Howe).

*

To account for seepage. In yet another version of Echo's story, the fifth-century poet Nonnos describes a scene in which Zeus has flooded the earth, and Pan scours the mountaintops for traces of Echo, who had long escaped his grasp but could—prior to the flood—still be heard singing in valleys and caves. "I fear the great flood may have covered her," Pan broods. "She has left the hills and moves restless over the waves. Echo once the maid of the rocks will show herself as the maid of the waters."

In almost every instance Echo slips her body into sound, evading capture. Across the forty-eight volumes of Nonnos' *Dionysiaca* she is frequently alluded to, but almost always from afar; she remains outside the frame, in the margins, in too many places at once to be captured by any god or narrative device.

*

Practiced breath in circular oceans. Tides form a net of shifting contact, moonpull. Stretch marks bloom in the space between soundings. Tilt glass to intercept the speech of light.

*

Only two species of flying birds are known to echolocate: the nocturnal, fruit-eating oilbird of South America, and the *Aerodramus* and *Collocalia* genera of the swiftlet family. Both species nest in dark caves, using echolocation to gather information about their surroundings and, in the case of oilbirds, forage palm and laurel fruit at night. Unlike most bats, the acoustic signals of these birds fall within a sonic range audible to human ears. The high-pitched clicking noises are produced by vibrating the exhalatory airflow as it passes through the birds' vocal organs in quick muscular contractions.

*

Gather mosses, eggshells. Cast-out signals extract echoes from the dark. Connective sinew re-percussions, Echo lashes out like latches clasping and unclasping, swiftlets clicking circuits in the trees. Gaia, limping, hides her pieces in the hills, unsettled Place talks back. Sounding out the phonemes of relation, atrophying diagrams of touch.

*

The voice gathers wood. Leaves flicker belly-up to signal coming storms. Echo touches the ground with both hands then rises. Backwards through trees, turns, forgetting. Mouth rearranged to the wind

an evening

rough glow
of window coins
in crescents

creaking
trees along
the shore

sleep comes often to me now

sea-legged

and holy

no one sees
the hunting dogs
I take for voice

poured ashes
over boat edge

lilac

    fish food

steals up through broken images

     what I wanted was

     to hold the sound
     against my tongue

     prolong the ridge

     between a voice

     and since

a numb limb shimmers

tongue's soft
node to battery

at its farthest limit every
boundary is an orifice

erosion of a wave
the length of clavicles

endangered corals
roped-off

net scrapes
shoreline

       no such
       thing as
       silence

sensitively

to write from
the body's

disrepair

vowels double
jointed

names we forge or forage

    simulate a
    sense of being
    carried without
    touch

we've grown fibrous
in our longing

broken
trees (lightning)

CDs hung from strings
to deflect sparrows

silence comes apart
in echo patchworks

smell of balsam   coiled
bud of navel

intolerable
smoothness of

without

made my way softly

remembered cardinal
points

tuning

sought no
permission to mourn

reef sounds

soft
erosion of
the mouth

in loam turned
brackish *oikos*

ash

plinth moon

connective twigs

test the edge of
objects ringing

       sheets of
       pattered tin

       .
       .
       .
       .

recalling just the outer
rings of what was lost

to separate a self
from signals

concave

       sea
       mouth recedes

slow moiré

of oil along
the coast

turned westward
driftwood

tangled in the vines

opal white
burls or emptied
branches

property delayed
by shifting echoes

unnamed touch-
stones sunken

ridge or lapis vein

undoes its offering

surface in
delay   abraded

rivulets of power
lines cut

shadows though
the trees

inhabitable

tension to dissemble
held in hips in

jaw
line irresolute
in storms

we re-emerge
as other sounds

striations of a wave
as measured flood as

glossaries in mica

held in diaphragm

shiver of an oilbird

(clicking) moonless

ground soaked with voices

cords of mist across

circumference grasses

run the seam of shore

INLET

1.

the voice pours out from sound
to organize the space around it

noise of rain and hair fall   wild rotation light

I brush my hair slowly in the silence formed between two mirrors

to see in all directions
                              deficit of nations

overgrown with roots and choral

2.

do we write in mourning for or forfeit of our selves?

my body, which is not only mine, spreads away
the more malleable space, like a swimmer

I press my palms against your stomach like a door

to sense the haptic darkness

to pour my inconclusions into shapes that I can hold

3.

hours host our bodies' dissolution

forest deep with haloes   wildfire

          fragrance held in air

before the lights came on
our eyes were freckled darkness before
sounds took shape
we were angels in an archway
pierced with long and diligent thorns

4.

the great barrier
reefs began to glow
before they died "phosphorescent
sunscreen" my new
immunities are costly

after the illness comes the holy feeling

image of a woman braced
with one foot on a boat the other
fixed ashore

5.

cold spoon
pressed to lower
cortex

the moths living in the kitchen
are mostly powder

with the lights off   moonlike

august turns upon us one half glistening

softened trash between the darker trees

"to make a habit of loss"
and losing   blurry hands pouring water
over forearms in a dream

ceiling shadow bruising into aura

6.

slip your body sideways between scaffolds

crossing shadows pitch blue
depth of metal

if duration is the width of attention held in place
we must drain the saltwater from stones
to make a tunnel

7.

to follow, to come following

echoic center of the after
image splits off into pupils

soft lung of fallen light on the roadside

what can't be seen we translate
into other vibratory matter

how the leap from one
orbit to another deletes time

8.

there are forms our bodies take
outside the image

small moon greenish

coin an iris
pressed into the subway platform

in my dream you held your hands over my eyes
and in them I saw separate darknesses

shards of compact
mirror shimmer   cisterns

flood beneath the tongue

9.

what's changing isn't time but the shapes that hold it

"shimmering field of the body" momentary
loss of vision

I drop my fingers into silent
pools of condensation on the table

the inner earth
the inner ear keeps
balance

you are leaning on the doorframe
bag of grapefruits propped upon your hipbone like a child

NOTES

Crane

p. 5: Ovid, *Fasti*, trans. Sir James George Frazer.

p. 7: Emily Dickinson, *Selected Letters*, ed. Thomas H. Johnson.

p. 8: Text adapted from the entry for "Cardo" in Charlton T. Lewis, *A Latin Dictionary*.

p. 9: Adapted from the entry for "κράδη," in Liddell & Scott, *A Greek–English Lexicon*.

p. 10: Ovid, *Metamorphoses*, trans. A.S. Kline.

p. 11: Anne Carson, "Essay on What I Think About Most," in *Men in the Off Hours*.

p. 13: Another translation of "κράδη," in *A Greek–English Lexicon*.

p. 17: Macrobius, *Saturnalia*, trans. Robert A. Kaster; Augustine, *Fathers of the Church*, trans. Demetrius B. Zema and Gerald G. Walsh; Tertullian, *On Idolatry*, trans. S. Thelwall. Thank you to Daniel Heller-Roazen, by way of Susan Howe, for directing me to the Tertullian quote.

p. 19: Roland Barthes, *The Neutral*, trans. Rosalind Kraus and

Denis Hollier; Barthes, "Death of the Author," trans. Stephen Heath.

p. 21: Barthes, *The Neutral*.

p. 24: Susan Buck-Morss, *Year 1*; The Barthes quote is adapted from a line in *Mythologies*, which reads in full: "But there always remains, around the final meaning, a halo of virtualities where other possible meanings are floating: the meaning can almost always be *interpreted*."

p. 25: Nathaniel Mackey, *Discrepant Engagement: Dissonance, Cross-Culturality and Experimental Writing*.

p.27: Roger Caillois, "Mimicry and Legendary Psychasthenia," trans. John Shepley.

Delay Figure

p. 37: Ovid, *Metamorphoses*, trans. Charles Martin.

p. 38: Édouard Glissant, *Poetics of Relation*, trans. Betsy Wing; Deborah Kapchan, "body," in *Keywords in Sound*, ed. David Novak and Matt Sakakeeny.

p. 39: "Orphic Hymn 11 to Pan," trans. Taylor, via *Theoi Greek Mythology*; Longus, *The Pastorals, or the Loves of Daphnis and Chloe*, trans. The Athenian Society.

p. 40: Glissant, *Poetics of Relation*; Amanda Weidman, "voice," in *Keywords in Sound*.

p. 42: Gilles Deleuze and Felix Guattari, *A Thousand Plateaus: Capitalism and Schizophrenia*, trans. Brian Massumi.

p. 44: Mackey, "Cante Moro," in *Paracritical Hinge*; Longus, *The Pastorals, or the Loves of Daphnis and Chloe*.

p. 45: Mark M. Smith, "echo," in *Keywords in Sound*; David Wills, quoted from a panel discussion in the symposium "*Prosthesis*: 25 years on," with Michael Naas and John Cayley at Brown University, November 2021 (transcribed by the author); Susan Howe, *Debths*.

p. 46: Nonnus, *Dionysiaca*, trans. W. H. D. Rouse; Signe Brinkløv, M. Brock Fenton, and John M. Ratcliffe, "Echolocation in Oilbirds and Swiftlets."

Inlet

p. 71: "to make a habit of loss" is an echo of Stacy Szymaszek's "help me to understand loss/ as a way of life," in *Three Novenas*.

p. 75: Barthes, *The Neutral*.

Acknowledgements

Thank you to the editors of *The Swan, Slow Poetry in America, digital vestiges,* and *SOME,* where excerpts from *Crane* first appeared, and to Carrie O. Adams and Janaka Stucky at Black Ocean for your belief in this project.

Deep gratitude to the friends and mentors who've helped grow this work, especially Cole Swensen, Samson Stilwell, Astrid Terrazas, Alex MacKay, Hamish Ballantyne, Sean McCoy, Claire Crews, Chloe Zimmerman, Sawako Nakayasu, Thangam Ravindranathan, and David Wills. To my mothers, Nancy Bolsover and Elizabeth Metcalf. To Susan Howe, for your guidance, wisdom, and friendship. And to M Cavuto, endlessly.